ISBN 978-0-428-36892-0
PIBN 11304952

1 MONTH OF
FREE
READING

at

www.ForgottenBooks.com

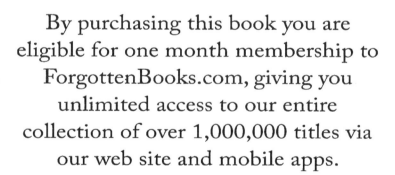

By purchasing this book you are
eligible for one month membership to
ForgottenBooks.com, giving you
unlimited access to our entire
collection of over 1,000,000 titles via
our web site and mobile apps.

To claim your free month visit:

www.forgottenbooks.com/free1304952

The 1983 Quittapahilla staff invites you to join us in viewing "The World is a Stage." The play, recounting the 1982-83 school year at Lebanon Valley College, is about to unfold. Each page contains several scenes from this memorable year. We apologize for the lack of a popcorn stand for this school premiere.

 Faculty

 Seniors

 Campus Living

 Organizations

 Greeks

 Sports

The students at LVC play the parts of main characters with a supporting cast of faculty and administration. The stage is life itself with scenes from the campus of LVC.

During Homecoming, all
the actors are on stage to
perform a scene of busy
and competitive action; as
in sports, parades, music
and productions.

THE
MOUSETRAP
by Agatha Christie

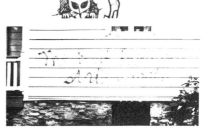

HOMECOMING COURT

The Homecoming Queen for this year's stage performance was Monika Stickel, with her court of Colleen Cassidy, Sue Newman, Susan Yeiter, Tammi Reynolds and Ann Sumner.

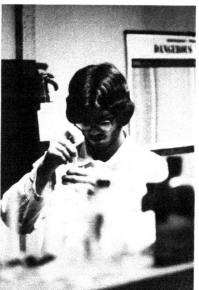

Cabaret

Some special actors in this play of life were on stage for special entertainment productions. A round of applause for those actors who worked hard on their extra performances.

This book is dedicated to

The Pajama G

ONE ACTS

Spring
Arts

Spring Arts Weekend
was another scene in this
play of life. Many
displayed their talents
through crafts, music and
clowning. Even previous
actors from earlier years
(alumni) came and played
their parts in this scene.
This weekend was a part
of the play that few can
say was boring.

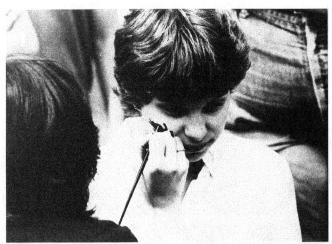

The Snow of '83

This was the year tradition came back. Approximately two feet of snow fell on February 11, blanketing the area with a white cover. Tradition came back on Sunday night, when snow mysteriously piled in front of all academic doors. (Mysteriously constitutes over 300 students shoveling and wetting snow in front of the doors.) Several people were slightly upset; but the general consensus was that it was the best attended campus activity in a while and it was fun. Watch out LVC for future snow storms and their consequences.

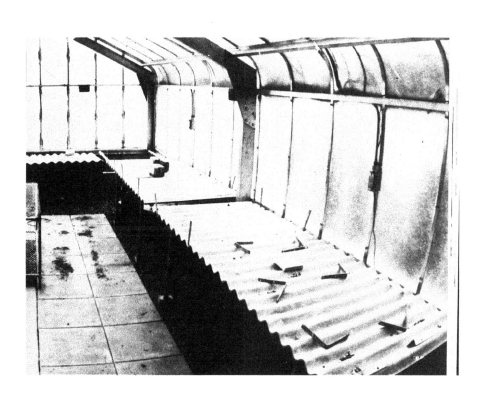

Adminis-
tration

Dr. Frederick P. Sample: President

Mary Eshleman

Dean Reed

Carol Schaak, Dean Yuhas, Dean Marquette, Dave Evans,
Pat Schools, Sue Carli.

THE LAUGHLIN HOUSE CREW — Harold Ulmer, Polly
Ehrgood, Carol Lennox, Peg Umberger, Marilyn Boeshore,
Helen Miller, Bob Unger.
Financial Aid: Christine Koterba, Marsha Hartmoyer
Business Office: Dr. Robert Riley, Barbara Smith, Arlene
Singer, Jackie Showers, Dane Wolfe
Admissions: Cathy Harky, Dean Greg Stanson, Bill Brown,
Donna Brown

MAINTENANCE — Row 1: Charles Ryland, Troy Matthew, Louis Cook, Bi
Rothermel, Harry Lane, Boyd Martin. Row 2: Lorie Hilton, Della Neidig, Bett
Brandt, Polly Long, Elsie Neefe, Dot Unger. Row 3: Carl Steiner, Charles Firestone
Vern Blair, Leon Yeiser, Jim Mimmersir.

Julie Woods, Christine Hopple, Doris Gerlach, Eloise Brown, William Hough, Alice Diehl, Grace Morrissey, Chaplain Smith, John Uhl.

Art

Dr. Richard
A. Iskowitz

Biology

Dr. Alan Wolfe, Dr. Paul Wolf, Dr. Ann
Henninger, Dr. Sidney Pollack.

Chemistry

Dr. Howard Neidig. Richard Bell, Dr.
Owen Moe, Dr. Donald Dahlberg.

Business Administration and Economics

Dr. Alan Heffner, Mr. David Seitz, Mr.
Kevin Reidy, Dr. C. F. Joseph Tom, Dr.
William Foeller, Mr. Richard Stone, Mr.
David Witmer.

Dr. Michael Grella, Dr. Madelyn
Albrecht, Mrs. June Herr, Dr. Eugene
Jacques.

Education

Dr. Leon Markowicz, Dr. Arthur Ford,
Glenn Woods, Dr. John Kearney, (below)
Dr. Philip Billings.

Histor
Scien

Foreign
Language

Dr. Dwight Page, Mrs. Helga
Dupont, Dr. James Scott, Dr.
Diane Iglesias.

Math

History and Political Science

Dr. Richard Joyce, Dr. John Norton, Dr. Elizabeth Geffen.

Dr. Joerg Mayer, Dr. Bryan Hearsey, Fay Burvas, Dr. Tousley.

Mathematics

Musi

Mr. Leonard Geissel, Mr. Ronald Bur-
richter, Mr. Robert Smith, Mr. William
Fairlamb, Dr. Robert Lau, Mr. Philip
Morgan, Dr. Leonard Getz, Dr. Dennis
Sweigart.

Musi

Philosophy

Dr. John Heffner, Dr. Carl Ehrhart

Roger Carlson

44

Physics

Dr. Jacob Rhodes, Dr. Robert O'Donnell, Dr. Barry Hurst.

Psychology

Dr. Roger Carlson, Dr. David Lasky, Dr. Robert Davidon, Dr. Jean Love.

Religion

Dr. Voorhis Cantrell, Dr. Elbert Wethington, Dr. Donald Byrne.

Sociology

Dr. Robert Clay, Dr. Howard Raiten, Dr. Carolyn Hanes,
other specialists.

Wanted: Male Actor

David J. Allen
Business Administration
Gladstone, NJ

Kurt D. Amlung
Business Administration
Westwood, NJ

Susan E. Bagley
Music Education
Salem, NJ

Stephen W. Beecher, Jr.
Psychology
Social Service
Chester, NJ

Norman J. Bell, Jr.
Economics
German
Lancaster, PA

David P. Beppler
Accounting
Penn Sauken, NJ

Brian W. Billies
Business Administratio
Oradell, NJ

Audrey L. Birkland
Elementary Education
Belle Mead, NJ

Karen A. Breitenstein
Medical Technology
Haworth, NJ

Susan J. Brewer
Operations Research
Newark Valley, NY

Lori E. Brown
Biology
Harrisburg, PA

Tad A. Brown
Social Service
Emmaus, PA

Thomas S. Brumbaugh
Business Administration
Lansdowne, PA

Victoria E. Bryden
English
Psychology
Bloomsburg, PA

William N. Campbell
Actuarial Science
Baltimore, MD

Colleen M. Cassidy
Computer Science
Oley, PA

Catherine C. Clarke
Music Education
Virginia Beach, VA

Julie M. Clay
Psychology
Harrisburg, PA

Kimberly A. Colvin
Social Service
Lebanon, PA

Jeffrey W. Conley
Accounting
Cordova, MD

Laurie A. Cook
Elementary Education
Mechanicsburg, PA

Theresa L. Cottrell
Medical Technology
Reading, PA

Actor watching murder-mystery play

Nancy M. Darnell
Social Service
Kennett Square, PA

Susan L. Davison
French
Freehold, NJ

Debra M. Decker
Biology
Delhi, NY

Mary A. DeHaven
Mathematics
Business Administration
Downingtown, PA

Peter A. Donnelly
Physics
South Plainfield, NJ

Debra D. Dunn
Political Science
English
Cinnaminson, NJ

Suzanne R. Duryea
Elementary Education
Chester, NJ

Debra S. Egolf
Chemistry
Mathematics
Carlisle, PA

Linda J. Evans
Mathematics
Music
Lansdowne, PA

John Feaster
Business Administration
Paramus, NJ

Sharon L. Ford
English
Trenton, NJ

Christopher W. Forlano
Music Education
Hatboro, PA

Garry M. Freysinger
Business Administration
New Cumberland, PA

Joy Furlong
Business Administration
Whitehouse Station, NJ

Kathy R. Gould
Accounting
Business Administration
Conowingo, MD

Actor meets cast

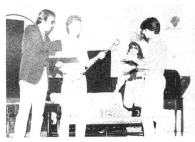
"You're the killer, so take the weapon."

Edward M. Grant
Business Administration
Kennett Square, PA

Anthony F. Guasperini
Business Administration
Aston, PA

David J. Hall
Psychology
Springfield, PA

Penny E. Harris
Social Service
Silver Spring, MD

Patricia L. Hassall
Music Education
Norristown, PA

Ramona S. Harwick
Social Service
Elizabethtown, PA

Susan H. Herald
Elementary Education
Highspire, PA

Gail E. Holdcraft
Accounting
Mt. Pleasant, SC

Victoria A. Holzman
Nursing
Laureldale, PA

Dawn C. Humphrey
English
West Pittston, PA

Thomas B. Jameson
Music Education
Woodstock, NY

Melanie A. Jones
Social Service
Psychology
Fallston, MD

David E. Kerr
Actuarial Science
Washington, NJ

Kay Koser
Chemistry
Elizabethtown, PA

"Now sneak up to the victim."

Uh-Oh! Trouble in the theater.

David A. Kramer
Economics
Cranbury, NJ

Joseph F. Krolczyk
Accounting
Baltimore, MD

Roger L. Kurtz
Sacred Music
Leola, PA

Debra M. Kus
Biochemistry
Warren, NJ

Kathryn L. Landis
Elementary Education
Akron, PA

Michael W. LaPorta, Jr.
Elementary Education
Hellertown, PA

Susan E. Lavery
Elementary Educatio
Psychology
Birmingham, AL

Joanne I. Lazzaro
Music Education
Spanish
High Falls, NY

Clifford L. Leaman
Music Education
Brownstown, PA

Gary R. Lehman
Accounting
Lebanon, PA

Robert E. Lemke
Accounting
Business Administrati
Smithtown, NY

58

Tina M. Liek
Religion
York, PA

Christopher D. Long
Accounting
Lebanon, PA

Kimberly J. Long
International Business
Sharon Hill, PA

Deborah M. Lucas
Psychology
Marysville, PA

Karen L. Lutz
Political Science
Reinerton, PA

Nicholas E. Magrowski
Music Education
Shillington, PA

Christopher M.
McArdle
Business Administration
Cheshire, CT

Margaret A. Michaels
Nursing
East Stroudsburg, PA

Malik N. Momin
Chemistry
Harrisburg, PA

Gregory B. Monteith
Business Administration
Ramsey, NJ

"You're supposed to stab her."

59

David L. Moyer
Physics
Myerstown, PA

Kimberly A. Mulder
German
Social Service
Parsippany, NJ

Tara Myers
Sociology
Millersville, PA

Drake E. Neimeyer
Psychology
Fogelsville, PA

Trouble lurks behind stage.

Stephen J. Nickerson
Accounting
Bel Air, MD

F. Darlene Olson
English
Gainesville, GA

Jesse E. O'Neill
Elementary Education
Chester, PA

Pamela M. Patton
Humanities
French
Bethesda, MD

Rebecca J. Powell
Elementary Education
Camp Hill, PA

Susan A. Purgert
Elementary Education
Psychology
Camp Hill, PA

Sharon M. Reeves
Elementary Education
Booton, NJ

Sandra L. Reisinger
Sociology
Sciotsville, OH

"Stop!"

Tamara L. Reynolds
Accounting
Madison, NJ

Frank S. Rhodes
Actuarial Science
Malvern, PA

Jeffrey S. Riehl
Music Education
Costa Mesa, CA

Ronald W. Robb
Business Administration
Pennsauken, NJ

Keith T. Roden
Music Education
Shiremanstown, PA

Lights out

J. Stuart Rose
Physics
Baltimore, MD

Richard B. Saltzer
Mathematics
German
Pottstown, PA

Anita M. Scheirer
Music
Catasauqua, PA

Bradley A. **Shatinsky**
Social Service
Laceyville, PA

Kimberly L. Sheffey
Spanish
International Business
Birdsboro, PA

Derick D. Shoff
Business Administration
Red Lion, PA

Michael W. Sigman
Religion
Lancaster, PA

Kathi L. Simms
Biology
Petersham, MA

Lynette M. Sottile
Social Service
Scranton, PA

Monika M. Stickel
Business Administration
Philosophy
Warren, NJ

Keith W. Sweger
Music Education
Columbia, PA

Matthew S. Thompson
Business Administration
Stillwater, NY

Brian C. Trust
Mathematics
Fallston, MD

Randall C. Valone
Economics
Business Administration
Longhorne, PA

Kevin J. Varano
Accounting
Elysburg, PA

Who's killing who?

Victor D. Viggiano
Business Administration
Franklin Lakes, NJ

Christopher J. Wachter
Actuarial Science
Kinnelon, NJ

Lauren S. Weigel
Music
Manchester, PA

Robert J. Wilhelm
Political Science
Lebanon, PA

Jane L. Wise
Biology
Martindale, PA

Lisa A. Wixted
Biochemistry
Williamstown, PA

Marilyn A. Wolfe
Accounting
Jonestown, PA

Susan J. Yeiter
Elementary Education
Woodbury, NJ

Lucy A. Zerbe
Music Education
Cherry Hill, NJ

Thomas L. Zimmerman
Actuarial Science
Intercourse, PA

Dawna H. Baker
English
Spring Grove, PA

James C. Bezanson
Mathematics
Business Administration
Freehold, NJ

Diane L. Heinz
Biology
Pittsburgh, PA

Twila M. Maust
Social Service
Lebanon, PA

Darryl L. Roland
Music
Business Administration
Palmyra, PA

Ann I. Seal
Biology
Scranton, PA

Michael L. Seigworth
English
Religion
Narminster, PA

Ann B. Sumner
Nursing
Willingboro, NJ

Patricia F. Weber
Social Service
Newton, NJ

65

Senior Superlatives

Girl Most Likely to Succeed	Bonnie Davenport
Guy Most Likely to Succeed	Brian Trust
Best Dressed	Monika Stickel
Worst Dressed	Rick Astor
Cutest Couple	Kay Koser and Frank Rhodes
Most Typical College Student	Chris Palmer
Best Body	Monika Stickel
Most Innocent	Marilyn Wolfe
Biggest Tease	Susan Lavery
Most Out of Touch With Reality	Colleen Cassidy
Best School Spirit	Susan Yeiter
Most Intellectual	Brian Trust
Quietest	Sue Purgert
Best Personality	Ann Sumner
Most Unique Laugh	Tom Myers
Most Preppy	Dave Allen
Biggest Gossip	Clio Girls
Class Space Cadet	Joanne Groman
Class Clown	John Feaster
Best Voice	Lauren Weigel
Most Talkative	Mary Dehaven
Best Athlete	Pete Donnelly
Best Actor	Rik Saltzer
Most Confused	Deb Dunn
Best Class	Class of '83

Who's Who Among Students in American Universities and Colleges

Colleen Marie Cassidy
Jeffrey Wayne Conley
Bonnie Sue Davenport
Michele LaRue DePrefontaine
Deborah Dee Dunn
Debra Sue Egolf
Sharon Lynn Ford
Dawn Claire Humphrey
Melanie Ann Jones
David Emerson Kerr
Kay Louise Koser
David Alan Kramer
Joanne Irene Lazzaro
Clifford Lynn Leaman
Christopher David Long
Thomas Gerald Myers
Susan Michelle Newman
Susan Ann Purgert
Frank Scott Rhodes
Jeffrey Scott Riehl
Susan Elaine Smith
Keith Warren Sweger
Brian Craig Trust
Marilyn Ann Wolfe
Elaine Ruth Woodworth

"Wanted: Male Actor"

Call the termite exterminator.

made for commercial purposes where
was greater, there was a tendency for t
man to prefer commercial investme
money-lending, certainly all banks i
commercial loans and the banker avoi
brium levelled at the pawnbroker and t
lender This creative diversion of inve
____ ther than into the support of cons____
____er, by the uncreative diversion of
____ with foreign exchange, another c
____ of making a profit The atmospher
____on these choices was charged not s
actual prosecution as by the case with
dodge his obligations through invoking
usury laws.

This atmosphere was compa____
Florence small money lenders th____
acce____ to the sacraments and Christ____
citizens of any substance had hold____
solidated public debt which paid in____
in it When the Lippomani ba____
Pisdi himself a merchant and ba____
were of such quality and ____ ____
and honoured in Venice that som____
they are arrested imprison____ ____
moral of these events whis____ ____
things is in the end deceived, th____

Health Center

Margaret Michaels, Mrs. Wolfe, Sue Thompson.

1st Floor
Row 1: Paula Fletcher, Darlene Snavely, Barbara Holden, Renea Linton, Robinne LeFever, Smurf, Terri Eastwood, Dicksie Boehler. Row 2: Audrey Huey, Margo Snow, Ruth Robinson, John Wood, Brenda Norcross, (Sharon Bear), Gloria Pochekailo, Debra Decker, Linda Iannucci, Doug Quaintance, Karen Milliken. Row 3: Robin Hammel, Rose Koch, Deb Chopko, Kelly Kefford, Mary Karapandza, Lisa Mason.

2nd Floor

Row 1: Barb Bereschak, Beryl Metz, Sue Butler. Row 2: Betty McLaughlin, Mary Foth, Jane Conley, Nancy Zerbe, Julie Farris, Becky Wise, Debbie Kohler, Diana Carey. Row 3: Anne Herald, Nancy Arciosky, Sue Kretovich, Patti Weber, Wendy Kauffman, Joann Lefever, Kris Van Benschoten, Lisa Edwards. Row 4: Lois Kaslow, Sue Light, Carolyn Dickerson, Alison Schiller, Tammy Reynolds, Karen Lutz, Sis Sottile, Lisa Wixted, Lori Herman, Anita Scheirer.

3rd Floor

Row 1: Lind Emerson. Row 2: Amy Abbott, Vicki Bryden, Mindy Cassel, Ruth Anderson, Julie Clay, Andrea Hue, Dawn Adams. Row 3: Arlene Loyd, Lisa Goetz, Janet Scratchley, Sheri Casciano, Anne Goodfriend, Cathy Singleton. Row 4: Faith Barnard, Cathy Bushyager, Daphne Kelloway, Chris Mosso, Margaret Brown, Cathy Conners. Row 5: Lorrie O'Brien, Chris Himmler, Sharon Carpenter, Laurie McKanna, Mary Karapanza, Robin Hammill. Row 6: Sandi Reisinger, Mary McNamera, Laurie Kratzer, Lisa Mason, Cora Bretz.

Mary Capp Green

75

Centre Hall

Row 1: Heidi (Lush) Wolfgang, Deb Dunn. Row 2: Colleen Costello, Marilyn Wolfe, Pam Kramer, Pat Hassel, Linda Evans, Colleen Cassidy. Row 3: Veronica Devitz, Gail Holdecraft, Joy Furlong, Ann Marcinkowski, Mary DeHaven, Lucy Zerbe.

Vickroy

1st Floor

Row 1: Patty Creasy, Nicole Collier, Maria Adessa, Kathy Bell, Ruth Kammerle. Row 2: Lori Yanci, Tracy Wenger, Debbie Howard, Julia Wilson, Julie Sealander, Lynn Cornelius, Amy Hastetler. Row 3: Melissa Horst, Lori Amendolara, Jean Grody, Helen Guyer, Betsy Warner, Wendy Carter, Maria Tursi, Kari Littlewood, Heidi Neuhoff, Leslie Paillex, Angela Carter. Row 4: Beth Ruoss, Holly Smith, Kathy Gillich, Alpha Johnson, Jane, Louise Brandeau, Kim Long. Row 5: Lori Brown, Deb Lucas, Janet Brown, Lisa Stahl, Joann Janewski, Deb Orndorff.

2nd Floor

Leslie Hall, Alison Verrier, Karen Ruliffson, Terri Roach, Deb Greene, Linda Stockhaus, Sandy Dahlstrom, Nina Nasiuta, Tami Mayo, Kate Rohland, Jean Krieg, Kathy Hostetter, Susan Cuddeback, Helinah Muniu, Lisa Mercado, Mary Beth Cook, Deb deArrastia, Michele Van Horn, Carla Giachero, Mindy Smith, Janet Sacco, Chris Karman, Tina Williams, Jean Doan, Vicki Frey, Jeanne Daly, Sara Bartlett, Hope Garling.

3rd Floor

Row 1: Janell Trexler, Denise Mastovich, Theresa Rachuba, Mary Seitz. Row 2: Rhonda Beekman, Cheryl Green, Louise Burchill, Lynn Wildonger, Megan Evans, Mel Herman, Sara Wardell, Diane Hafner, Martha Sipe. Row 3: Sandy Hiser, Jennifer Weiler, Lisa Myers, Deanna Metka, Ann Seal, Irene Hopper, Kim Davis, Marie Cinquanto, Michele Morel. Row 4: Sheila McElwee, Ann Wise, Sondra Watson, Patty Houseknecht, Deb Patterson, Kathi Simms, Mary Ann Burkland, Elisabeth Garner.

Silver

Basement
Row 1: Carol Bennedick, Amy Ziegler, Annett Schwind.
Row 2: Barbara Nace, Jody Collier, Peggy Leister, Cheryl
Kaufman. Row 3: Susan Jones, Deb Egolf, Kim Catino,
Holly Smith. Row 4: Elaine Hoilman, Chris Dengler,
(Tony), Cindy Nolt, Heidi Bass.

1st Floor
Row 1: Darlene Olson, Ramona
Harwick, Lois Graff, Michele
Hoffman. Row 2: Sue Brewer, Sue
Newman, Rhoda Mugunda, Maria
Montesano, Michelle Glascow.
Row 3: Diane McVaugh, Tina
Liek, Jan Brown, Lois Hagerman,
Linda Lentz, Tammy Rowe. Row 4:
Sharon Reeves, Lisa Harrison,
Suzanne Duryea, Pam Patton,
Donna Reeves, Charley.

2nd Floor

Row 1: Wendy Kahn, Jane Buscaglia, Sandi Burke, Joanne Lazarro, Karen Bixler, Melanie Jones. Row 2: Michele Gawel, Heather Walter, Betsy Gross, Barb Crall. Row 3: Kim Pearl, Jeanette Halterman, Ruth Carpenter, Rachel Clark. Row 4: Janell Macrie, Carol Davison, Leslie Gilmore, Julia Gallo-Torres, Virginia Lotz, Carol Neiman, Kim Mulder, Marcia Davis, Chris Vagyoczky. Row 5: Leeann Kohler, Kristi Barbatschi, Jill Murray.

3rd Floor

North College

Row 1: Amy Barefoot, Jeanne Page, Ann Buchman. Row 2: Becky Powel, Laurie Cook, Nancy Darnell, Brenda Focht, Kim McKenrick, Carol Dennison. Row 3: Sherri Becker, Rebecca Fisher, Audrey Birkland, Susan Yeiter, Ann Sumner, Leslie Engesser.

1st Floor
Row 1: Brian Billies, Pam Kramer, Garry Freisinger. Row 2: R. C. Vogel, Jed Duryea, Bill Campbell, Pete Vogel, Joe Rotunda, Mark Sutovich, Steve Weddle.

Keister

3rd Floor

Row 1: Steve Lenker, Jesse O'Neill, Joseph Schappell, Rich Hoffman, Eric (Duke) Shoen. Row 2: Michael Gillespie, Scott Martin, Stan Sullivan, Dave Williams, Jerry Wisniewski, Eric Kratzer, Bobby Daniels, Chris Rodes. Row 3: Keith Bruton, Jim Foster, Douglas Sernoffsky, Bill Stevenson. Row 4: Rich Miller, Frank Percelli, Rick Astor. Missing: Dave Ludwig, Jim Deer, Pat Zlogar, Rick Shoff, Dan Rafferty, Mark Clifford, Dwayne Martin, Dave Bedway, Marc Hess.

1st Floor

3rd Floor

Sheri

2nd Floor

1st Row: P. J. Keitock, Chris Roberts, Rich Underwood, Joe "Toad" Porterleis, James O'Neill, Tad Brown. **2nd Row:** Dave Barbush, Don Hanes, Chuck Beard, Mark Brewer, Chuck Fisher, Tom Steffanie, John "Boop" Deemer.

Row 1: Ray Rose, Chris Palmer, Lyle Trumbull, Paul Ruser, Mike Sigworth. Row 2: Nick Verrati. Row 3: Marty Werkheiser, John Ferrara, Dennis Delduco, Dan Delduco, Greg Goodwin, Jon Spotts, Bob Bryant, Jeff Ham.

Sheridan

Funkhouser
West

Basement

Row 1: Mike May, Bill Faylor, Tom Kane. Row 2: Dave Fishel. Row 3: Kevin Peters, Dave Withington, Martin McCabo, Jim Algeo, Tony Lamberto. Row 4: Drake Neimeyer, Art Hannah, Dan Capadano, Randy Herman, Brad Chance.

1st Floor

Row 1: Carl Dorsey, Bud Drake, Dave "Smokey" Frye, Geoff Howson, Jonathon Frye, Cliff Leaman, John Herr, Steve Garnier, Bob Fullenlove, Si Van Do. Row 2: Scott Inners, Dave Moyer, Pete Donnelly, Tom Zimmerman, Steve Nelson, Dave Hall, Frank Rhoads.

2nd Floor

Row 1: Tom Brumbaugh, Leather, John Keiffel, George Suede, Deb Kus, Tom Myers, Tim Hazelwood. Row 2: John Mount, Carl Muller, Bret Hershey, Todd Hrico, Jeff Beatty, Neill Keller, Earl Lambert, Dave Ebaugh, Al Weck, Bryan Achey, Bryan Hoke, Karl Gerlott, Jim Hollister, Jim Mount. Row 3: Tim Wolf, Dale Groome, George Reiner, Tim Niles, Chris Forlano, Keith Sweger, Ron Robb, Jim Ross, Greg Klinger, Bryan Hartman.

3rd Floor

Campus Living Cont. on Page 110

Row 1: Jeff Copeland, Brian Gockley, Steve Lefarge, Eric Enters, Nick Lacovara, Harold Vurrman. Row 2: Dale Croome, Tom Owsinski, Brian Trust, Cliff Plummer, Bob Bruno, Jeff Snyder, Steve Lefurge, Nick Magrowski, Craig Van Benschoten, Scott Phillips, John Washchysion, Don Pletcher.

Organizations

Class of '83

President: Jeff Conley, Secretary: Elaine Woodworth, Treasurer: Colleen Cassidy, Vice-President: SallyAnne Foose.

Class of '84

Secretary: Rebecca Fisher, Treasurer: Carol Dennison, President: Wayne Meyer, Missing: Vice-President: Mary McNamara.

Class of '85

President: Wendy Kauffman, Vice-President: Mary Seitz, Treasurer: Pam Beebe, Secretary: Lisa Edwards.

Class of '86

Vice-President: Denise Mastovich, President: Nicole Collier, Secretary: Tracy Wenger, Treasurer: Maria Tursi.

Student Council

Row 1: Heidi Bass (corresponding secretary), Rik Saltzer (recording secretary), Tammy Reynolds (president), Anthony Lamberto. Row 2: Brian Trust (treasurer), Lynn Cornelius, Wendy Carter (asst. treasurer), Susan Yeiter (social vice-president), Michelle Gawel, Mark Scott. Row 3: Jonathan Frye, Tad Brown, Karl Peckman, Jesse O'Neill, Ann Sumner (academic vice-president), Kenny Hendershot, Chris Monighan.

Susan Nolan, John Deemer, Vice-Chairman: Brian Cain, Chairman: Monika Stickel, Jane Ropert, Kay Bennighof, Lili Fisher, Julie Illick, Laurie Hittinger, Deanna Metka.

Row 1: Jane Rupert, Debra Kus, Mary Seitz. Row 2: Cliff Plummer, Mark George, Jonathan Frye.

CIB

Quitte

Mark Scott, Robin Hammell, Cheryl Green. Cora Bretz, Editor; Darlene Olson.

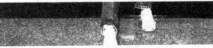

Quad

Sharon Ford, Features Editor; Dawn Humphrey, Layout Editor; Dave Frye, Managing Editor; Tracy Wenger, Sports Editor; Arthur Ford, Advisor; Lisa Meyer, Amy Hostetler, Associate Editor; Michele DePrefontaine, Copy Editor.

Spring Arts

Row 1: Coordinator: Rebecca Fisher, Betty McLaughlin, Renea Linton, Deb Chopko. Row 2: Assistant Coordinator: Judy Walter, Lynn Wildonger, Nancy Darnell, Veronica Devitz. Row 3: Carol Dennison, Kim Sheffey, Gloria Pochekailo, Paul Rusen. Row 4: Dean Sauder, Rhonda Beekman, Rose Koch, Audrey Birkland. Row 5: Treasurer: Brian Trust, Cheryl Kaufman, Kay Koser. Row 6: Bob Hurter, Marie Cinquanto, Kim Davis, Tim Niles. Row 7: Harold Haslett, Ken Neely, Heidi Neuhoff, Michelle Morel. Row 8: Sue Jones, Diane McVaugh, Tim Findon, Maria Adessa. Row 9: Bob Dirico, Julie Sealander, Jim Angerole.

Photo Club

Dave Ferruzza, President; Chris Palmer, Bill Moore, Toni Kazmierczak, Chris McArdle.

French Club

Row 1: Treasurer: JoAnne Stimpson. President: Pamela Patton. Vice-President: Michele DePrefontaine. Row 2: Terry Long. Secretary: Sue Davison.

Row 1: Bob Wilhelm, Norman Bell, Dave Ferruzza, Mark Scott. Row 2: Frau Dupont, Kristi Barbatschi, Brenda Focht, Herr Scott, Deanna Metka, Chris Jasman, Jack Thomas. JoAnne Stimpson.

German Club

Spanish Club

Row 1: Sue Lavery, Tom Kane, Lisa Meyers. Row 2: Joanne Lazzaro (pres.), Sheffy, Sue Davison, Barb Long, Rachel Clarke, Sandy Hiser.

International Relations Club

Mariann Shadel, Secretary, Toni Kazmiesczak, Mostafa Sheykhnazavi, Sheffey, Kimberly J. Long, President, Sue Davison, Publicity Czar, Helinch Nunin, Vice President, Chris McArdle.

Fellowship of Christian Athletes

Row 1: Kent Henry, Todd Burkhardt, Steve Nelson, Steve Garnier. Row 2: Wendy Carter, Brad Chance, Jenny Deardorf. Row 3: Deb Detwiler, Julie Sealander.

Project

Row 1: Barbara DeMoreland, Donna Kubik, Michele Glascow, Brad Chance, Rachael Clarke. Row 2: Chaplain Smith, Kent Henry, Steve Garnier, Patchel Landis, George Reiner. Cindy Nolt, Deb Dressler. Row 3: Chris Wachter, Kim Mulder (pres.), Darlene Olson, Melanie Jones. David Kramer.

WLVC

Row 1: Bruce Peterson, Vice-President; Kevin Bruck, Station Manager; Eric Smith. Row 2: Mark Scott, Bruce Hoffman, Bill Moore, Tammy Rowe, Carl Dorsey, Lois Graff, Lane Hess.

Row 1: Craig VanBenschoten, Seth Stone, Treasurer; John Brady, Lane Hess, President; Bob Wilhelm. Row 2: Deb Fullman, Rich Bradley, Bill Viverito, Sue Thompson, Marge Michaels, Bryan Hearsey, Dave Eckman. Row 3: Walt Fullman, Rob Frey, Ann Sehonic, Secretary; Dawn Adams, Lori Stone, Janet Brown, Chris Palmer.

Ski Club

97

Biology Club

Row 1: Lisa Stahl, Joanne Janeski, Deb Orndorf, Kathy Gillich, Joe Bonacquisti, Deb Lucas, Vice-President: Robin Hammell. Row 2: Treasurer: Ann Seal, Irene Hopper, Barry Sweger, President: Lori Brown, Kathi Simms, Wendy Kauffman, Sheila McElwee.

Row 1: Dan Delp, Jim Emphield, Leland Steinke, Rob Fry, George Reiner, Dave Blauch, Mostoufa Sheykhnozaki, Mark Witmer. Row 2: Kay Koser, Julie Stinner, Michele Glasgow, Cindy Nolt, Lily Fisher. Row 3: Judy Iskowitz, Deanna Metka, Deb Kus, Deb Egolf, Laurie Hittinger, Steve Rosier, Si Van Do.

Chemistry Club

Row 1: Ruth Anderson, Darryl Adler, Keith Hurst, Cheryl Green, Rhonda Beekman, Dave Kerr, Colleen Cassidy, Tami Mayo, Michele VanHorn, Sand Dahlstrom. Row 2: Cathy Conner, Ann Marcinkowski, Frank Rhodes, Barb Holden, Tom Zimmerman (treasurer), Mary DeHaven (secretary), Debbie Howard, Linda Stockhaus, Kay Bennighof (president). Row 3: Pat Kowalski, Rik Saltzer, Linda Evans, Brian Trust. Row 4: Scott Inners, Jim Stoltfus, Nancy Arciosky, Barb Bereschak, Bob Fager, Jeff Wieboldt, Rick Astor, Mary Seitz (vice-president), Bob Dirico.

Math Club

Row 1: Jean Krieg (president), Deb Greene (secretary), Marilyn Wolfe (vice-president). Row 2: Leslie Hall, Karen Ruliffson, Deb deArrastia, Joanne Janeski. Row 3: Pam Beebe, Audrey Huey, Barb Holden, Deb Chopko, Robinne Lefever, Lisa Edwards, Joann LeFever, Carolyn Dickerson, Cheryl Green, Michele Morel. Row 4: Peter Lunde, Mike Kelsall, Jeff Ham, Stephen Lefurge, Brian Trust, Kevin Varano, Stephen Nickerson, Rhonda Beekman, Sheffey. Row 5: Tom Stefany, Lois Kaslow, Louise Burchill, John Gebhard.

Childhood Ed Club

Row 1: Alison Daubert, Julie Farris, Jesse O'Neill (president), Lisa Harrison. Row 2: Mary Karapandza (vice-president), Susan Cuddeback, Kim Pearl, Lois Hagerman, Lois Graff, Carla Giachero, Margo Smith. Row 3: Ruth Robinson, Brenda Norcross, Amy Ziegler, Lori Yanci, Sue Purgert (secretary), Sharon (Rainbow) Reeves, Susan Smith (treasurer), Cindy Kramer, Patty Troutman, Mrs. Herr (advisor).

Psychology Club

Row 1: Vicky Bryden (president), Linda Emerson (vice-president). Row 2: Daphne Kellaway, Cathy Bushyager, Deb Lucas, Neill Keller.

Wig and Buckle

Brenda Norcross, Ruth Robinson, Chris Forlano, Keith Sweeger, Cora Bretz, Ann Marcinkowski, Sharon Ford, Laurie McKannan, Stephen Lefurge, Carol Benedick, Kent Henry, Barb Bereschak, Sue Nolan, Linda Evans, Deb Kus, Tom Meyers, Vickie Ulmer, Nancy Arciosky, Rik Saltzer, Amy Hostetler, Colleen Cassidy, Tom Jameson, Jeff Conley, Brian Trust.

H.I.S.

Duane Martin, Tom Jameson, Sharon Ford, Sue Lavery, Joanne Lazzaro, Allan Dutton, Bud Drake, Diane Detwiler.

MENC

Row 1: Holly Hanawalt (secretary), Barb Nace, Linda Iannucci, Lselie Engesser, Julie Illick, Gloria Ponchekailo, Diane McVaugh (president). Row 2: Cathy Clarke (vice-president), Bret Hershey, Jill Herman (treasurer). Heidi Nuehoff, Julie Gunshenan, Janell Trexler, Maria Adessa, Chris Enck, Scott Lefurge, Rose Koch, Mark Wagner, Vicki Frey, Jim Hollister. Row 3: Patty Houseknecht, Carol Jordan, Debra Patterson, Todd Hrico, Tim Niles, Tim Findon, Bryan Hartman, Melanie Herman, Betty McLaughlin, Winston Gray, Nick Magrowski, Jon Heisey, Jim Conzelmann, Judy Walter, Dean Sauder, Tom Owsinski, Dale Groome. Not Pictured: Sue Bagley, Joanne Groman, Pat Hassall, Joanne Lazarro, Jeff Riehl, Keith Sweger, Keith Roden, Steve Weber, Lucy Zerbe, Carol Anderson, Mary Jane Beazley, Jane Buscaglia, Jill Wenrich, Diane Detwiler, April Pelligrini, Sara Bartlett, Jeanne Daly, Carol Neiman, Brad Still.

Guild Student Group

Row 1: Betty McLaughlin, Laura Fowler, Holly Hanawalt, Barb Kramer. Row 2: Martha Sipe, Elisabeth Garner, John Overman, Carol Jordan, Mark Wagner, Joanne Groman (vice-president), Roger Kurtz (president), Tom Myers (sec./treas.), Tim Findon, George Reiner.

Concert Choir

Susan Eileen Bagley, Richard David Brode, Ann M. Buchman, Catherine Chiles Clarke, James R. Conzelmann, Diane Patricia Detwiler, Howard Russell Drake, Erik Lawrence Enters, Timothy Allen Findon, Laura Ann Fowler, Dorothy Diane Garling, Elizabeth June Gross, Diane Marie Hafner, Holly Jean Hanawalt, Jennifer Rean Hatcher, Jon Michael Heisey, Jill Eileen Herman, Melanie Dawn Herman, Bret Carl Hershey, Sandra Jean Hiser, James Harold Hollister, Linda A. Hostetter, Carol Miriam Jordan, Allan C. Junggust, Gregg William Klinger, Earl Dwayne Lambert, Susan Elizabeth Lavery, Thomas G. Myers, John Frederick Overman, Debra Lynne Patterson, April Joy Pellegrini, Harriet Doris Raunzahn, Jeffrey Scott Riehl, Terri Lynn Roach, Keith T. Roden, Darryl Lee Roland, Bryan G. Rowe, Wallace H. Umberger Jr., Mark Frederick Wagner, Heather Lee Walter, Steven Todd Weber, Julia Lynn Wilson, John Marshall Woods, Stephen Leonard Wysocki, Nancy Jean Zerbee, Director: Dr. Getz.

Wind Ensemble

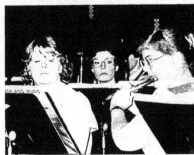

Sara Louise Bartlett, Heidi Susan Bass, Louise Suzanne Brandeau, Richard David Brode, Jane Nancy Buscaglia, Catherine Chiles Clarke, Jane Louise Conley, Jeanne Marie Daly, Christopher B. Enck, Leslie Engesser, Linda Jeanne Evans, Christopher W. Forlano, Mary Lynn Foth, Vicki Lynn Frey, Andrew F. Grider, Dale R. Groome, Patricia L. Hassall, Timothy Alan Hazelwood, Jon Michael Heisey, Jill Eileen Herman, Bret Carl Hershey, Laurie Rose Hittinger, Barbara Ried Holden, James Harold Hollister, Rick Joseph Hoffman, Gregg William Klinger, Rosalie Lou Koch, Joanne Irene Lazzaro, Clifford Lynn Leaman, Linda Marie Ludwig, Michael McDonald May, Elizabeth A. McLaughlin, Barbara Ann Nace, Heidi Lynn Neuhoff, Timothy Olin Niles, Thomas E. Owsinski, Gloria Marie Pochekailo, M. Dean Sauden, Curtis William Sipe, Melinda Susan Smith, Keith Warren Sweger, Janell Beth Trexler, Judith Louise Walter, Sara May Wardell, Sondra Lee Watson, Patricia Elise Whiteman, Director: Mr. Geissel.

Softball Club

Susan Smith, Diane Detwiler, Patty Houseknecht, Lisa Miele, Denise Mastovich, Deb Lucas, Terry Eastwood, Janet Brown.

Laughing Club?

Jazz Band

Saxophones: Curt Sipe (director), Dave Carter, Mike Hogan (business manager), Nick Magrowski, Chris Forlano; **Trombones:** Tim Wolf, Tom Owsinski, Dale Groome, Steve Nickerson, Mike May; **Trumpets:** Tim Niles, Allan Junggust, Chris Long, Mark Witmer, Jon Heisey; **Rhythm:** Gregg Klinger, Tony Sheffy, Dave Baldwin, Keith Sweger.

Marching Band

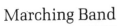

Basement

Row 1: Joe (Zep) Ruocco, Jim Bryant.
Row 2: Mike Rusen, Wib Elliot, Mark
Alexander, Linda Ludwig, Cheryl
Strong, Lynn DeWald, Joanna-Claire
Metz, Kevin Varano, Rob Ferrick, Steve
Beecher, A. J. Jung, John A. Dalton. Row
3: Terry Kimbel, Eric Trainer.

1st Floor

Row 1: Randy Valone, Ralph Acker-
man. Row 2: Jeff Bair, Wayne Martin,
Bob Wilhelm, Joe Rieg. Row 3: Scott
Pontz, Bob DiRico, Fred Siebecker,
Tony Meyers, Curt Keen, David Ferruz-
za, (Clark **Kent** Douglas **Henry** Aaron
Fir Jr.), Jeff Boland, Mike Kelsaw.

2nd Floor

Row 1: Bob Fager, Brad Shatinsky, Steve Rosier, Bob Fry. Row 2: David Richter, Harold Hasslet, Brad Still, Darryl Adler, Peter Lunde, Jay Hagerty, Stephen Sier, Jim Angerole. Row 3: James Budd, Dave Beppler.

3rd Floor

Row 1: David Kramer, Eric Smith, Bob Gross, Bruce Peterson. Row 2: Bob McGonigal, Jeff Bravman, Bob Hurter, Mustafa Sheykhnazari, Bruce Hoffman, John Brady, Allan Junggust, Thumper. Row 3: Mike Plank, John Lee, Dave Kurjiuka, Pete Johansson. Row 4: Terry Gusler, Terry Miller, Chris Wacter, Ken Neely, Joe Bonaquisti. Row 5: Kevin Bruck, Leland Steinke, Dan Delp, Steve Richter, John Woods.

117

Pi Gamma Mu

Row 1: Deb Detwiler, Kim Colvin, Dave Kramer, Cheryl Green, Mary Jean Bishop. Row 2: Nancy Darnell, Elaine Woodworth, Marilyn Wolfe, Jeff Conley.

Beta Beta Beta

Row 1: Diane Heinz, Robin Hammell. Row 2: Jonathan Frye, Cynthia Nolt, Si Van Do, Dave Carter, Wendy Kauffman, Jeanette Lasher, Carol Beredick. Row 3: Michele Glascow, Sue Eberly, Barry Sweigert, Rich Willis, Joe Bonaquista, Dr. Herringer.

Psi Chi

Row 1: Dr. Carlson, Karen Milliken (Pres.), Sue Purgert (V.P.), Kathy Bashere, Dr. Love. Row 2: Chris McArdle, Dr. Lasky (Adv.), Anne Vasallo, Ruth Carpenter, Becky Rotz.

Row 1: Bill Moore, Kevin Buck (V.P.). Row 2: Karen Bixler, Kari Littlewood, Donna Kubik, George Reiner. Row 3: Deb Detwiler (Sec.), Steve Nelson, Patchel Lands, Barb DeMoreland, Michele Glascow, Cendy Nolt, Chaplain Smith (Adv.). Row 4: Kim Mulder, Dave Kramer (Treas.), Melanie Jones (Pres.), Darlene Olson.

Delta Tau Chi

Gamma Sigma Sigma

Row 1: Michelle Morel, Judy Walter, Lori Yanci, Lynn Cornelios, Wendy Kauffman, Deb Detwiler, Kay Koser, Michelle DePrefontaine, Colleen Cassidy, Cindy Kramer. Row 2: Alison Daubert, Deb Lucas, Rose Koch, Marilyn Wolfe, Gloria Pochekailo, Lisa Edwards, Ann Seal, Irene Hopper, Beryl Metz, Nancy Darnell, Deb Kus, Patty Weber, Tammy Reynolds. Row 3: Deb Chopko, Kim Long, Deb Dunn, Lois Graff, Bonnie Davenport, Elaine Woodworth, Sue Bagley, Julie Stinner, Mary Jean Bishop, Karen Lutz, Carolyn Dickerson. Row 4: Brenda Norcross, Pat Kowalski.

Phi
Omega

OTHERS — Row 1: Mark Desimone, Dave Bouch, David Kramner, Kenny McKellar, Bill Moore, Steve Beecher. Row 2: Tom ne, John Dayton, Dave Carter, Cliff Plummer, Karl Gerlott, Jim Budd, Jeff Weibolt. Row 3: Brad Chance, John Heisey, Dave pler, Brian Trust, Steve Nickerson, Steve Lefurge, Bob Dirico, Fred Siebecker, Jay Haggerty, Kurt Kean. Row 4: Joe "Zep" Ruocco, tt Lefurge.
EDGES — Row 1: Harold Hasslett, Jim Angerol, Rich Britenstien. Row 2: Bruce Peterson, Scott Pontz, Jeff Boland, Konstantinos tzikowtelis or Gus, Erik Enters, Kent Henry, (Chicken), Dave Ferruzza. Row 3: Wib Elliott, Geoff Howsen, "Burt" Weck, Dave augh, Dave Bedway. Row 4: Joe Rieg, Bob Bruno. Missing: Mark Alexander, John Woods.

Phi Mu Alpha Sinfonia

Row 1: Jon Heisey, Rick Huffman, Earl Lambert, Bryan Hoke, Jim Hollister, Andy Grider, Tim Niles. Row 2: Gregg Klinger, Wally Umberger, Bret Hershey, Nick Magrowski, Bryan Hartman, Jim Conzelmann, Tim Findon, Chris Enck, Allan Junggust. Row 3: Tom Myers, Rich Brode, Mark Wagner, Todd Arico, Dean Sayder, Tom Jameson, John Overman, Dale Groome, Tom Owsinsky.

Sigma Alpha Iota

Row 1: Julia Wilson, Betty McLaughlin. Row 2: Sara Wardell, Kathy Bell, Mel Herman, Joanne Groman, Sara Bartlett, Elisabeth Garner, Holly Hanawalt, Cathy Clarke, Vicki Ulmer, Deb Patterson, Sondra Watson, Heidi Neuhoff. Row 3: Maria Adessa, Barb Nace, Julie Gunshenan, Martha Sipe, Lauren Weigel, Laurie McKannon, Jannell Trexler.

Knights of the Valley

Chris Palmer, Mike Sigworth, John Ferrara, Dennis Delduco, Paul Rusen, Bob Bryant, Ray Rose, Dan Delduco, Lyle Trumbull, Dave Eckman, Marty Werkheiser, "Ron," Nick Verrati, Jeff Ham, Greg Goodwin, Jon Spotts.

FRIENDS — Jim Bryant, Mike Rusen, Dave Fischel.

Delta
Lambda
Sigma

Row 1: Linda Emerson, Robin Hammell.
Row 2: Janet Scratchly, Daphne Kellaway,
Sharon Carpenter. Row 3: Mary
Karapandza, Faith Barnard, Joy Furlong,
Dawn Adams. Row 4: Julie Clay, Sandi
Reisinger, Chris Himmler, Laurie O'Brien,
Gail Holdcraft, Miriam Hudecheck, Amy
Abbott, Andrea Hue. Missing: Terri Hue,
Chris Mosso, Mary McNamara, Cathy
Bushyager.

Kappa Lambda Nu

Row 1: Susan Yitee, Laurie Cook, Sue Brewer, Audrey Birkland, Sue Newman, Ann Sumner. Row 2: Mary Foth, Jo Anne Janeski, Michelle Gawel, Leslie Gusciora, Terri Roach, Kyle Loehr, Kristi Barbatschi, Kate Rohland. Row 3: Jody Hatcher, Wendy Kahn, Carol Denison, Julia Gallo-Torres, Ann Buchman, Besty Gross, Heather Walter, Lisa Stahl, Helen Guyer, Becky Powell, Jeanne Page. Row 4: Virginia Lotz, Patti Mongon, Rebecca Fisher, Sherri Becker, Veronica Devitz, Amy Barefoot, Deb Orndorf, Leslie Hall.

Phi
Lamba
Sigma

y O'Hare, Bob Johnston, John Kiefel, Tony Sheffy, Charley Har-
h, John Gebhard.

Kappa Lambda Sigma

Alpha Psi Omega

Row 1: Linda Evans, Brian Trust, Rik Saltzer, Deb Kus, Dean Sauder, Vicki Ulmer. Row 2: Sharon Ford, Tom Jameson, Gail Holdcraft, Ann Marcinkowski, Mark Wagner. Row 3: Tom Myers, Laurie McKannan.

A Curtain Call

The world is a stage,
As the curtain does call,
— Actors all are we . . .
With masks and costumes and
    Scripts and all,
It is our reality . . .

The stage is set,
The overture starts,
The lights burst on . . . then fade . . .
The actors dance and please the world,
With the impressions they have made.

We play the stage
And laugh in time
As the curtain calls again . . .
Our lives are staged and set
in line, —
They are all remembered then.

Faces and masks are met and
shared,
Some are false and some made true,
We act open the lives we dare
All adventures welcome new . . .

The curtain arises now; Once more
— The lights go up — not as before . . .
The music starts — it's last to play
Before the actors bow their stay . . .

The world is a stage for us all,
We have the power to act or fall.
The music is ours, the light's on us,
We all are the actors in this age,
We must reach our limits and always live,
As if the world were a stage . . .
                For L. W.
                MA '83

Believer's Prayer

I believe in nature,
And the beauty of her ways,
I believe in sunshine,
That brightens up the days.
I oft' believe in silver clouds
And thunderous stormy nights.
I believe in wishing stars,
Their radiant faith; in light.
I believe in music.
As the language of us all,
I believe in loving friends,
To catch us if we fall.

I believe in rainbows,
With colors soft and bright,
— God's symbol to his people,
That we'll always see the light.
I believe in fairy tales,
With their lucky pots of gold.
I believe in memories,
That shall never seem too old.
I believe in poetry,
As the message of the heart,
With symbols bold,
And meanings strong,
Which never seems to part.

I believe in friendship,
And hurtful pathways there,
When I believe I know someone,
There, hurting will not care.
I often see, with observing eyes,
The truth told through lies,
I believe in miracles,
And faith that never dies . . .
I believe in myself,
And freaks of nature too,
But most of all, and of much concern,
I believe in you.

    For J. B.
    MA

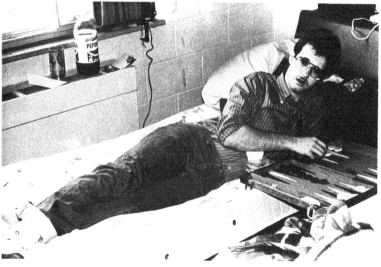

137

Soccer

Row 1: Victor Viggiano, Kurt Amlung, Greg Monteith (captain), Joe
Morrison, (captain), Bob Fullenlove, Rich Troutman. Row 2: Erik Enters,
Paul Gouza, Eigil Frost, John Naylor, Dan Capodanno, Scott Martin,
Mark Brewer. Row 3: Brian Gockley, Jed Duryea, Gus Hatzikoutelis,
Coach Correll, Jim Bryant, Dave Pesta.

Football

Row 1: Herb Hutchinson, Joe Schappell, Greg Weaber, John Feaster, Phil DePompeo, Jud Brown, Pete Donnelly, Steve Beecher, Rick Shoff, Dan Mills. Row 2: Bill Cambell, Rob Muir, Wayne Meyer, John Dayton, Nate Adams, Ed Fackler, Rob McCallian, John Brady, Bob Krasley, Kurt Musselman, Joe Lamberto. Row 3: Pete Vogel, John Deemer, Joe Rotunda, Marty McCabe, Nick Verratti, Jim Algeo, John Taormina, Karl Peckman, Doug Rickenbach, Tom Kane, Bernard Branch. Row 4: John Zappala, Rich Miller, Bill Stevenson, John Conners, Bob Bruno, Dave Gehret, Frank Purcell, Bob Carson, Mark Clifford, Kevin Peters, John Chupek. Row 5: Jim Bezanson (manager), Ann Sumner (student trainer), Harold Getz (asst. coach), Tom Kimmel (asst. coach), John DeFrank (asst. coach), Terence Kimble, John Washchysion, Dave Ludwig, Jim Gibbons (asst. coach), Kent Reed (defensive coordinator), Sharon Grissinger (trainer), Chris Bengler (student trainer), Brad Shatinsky (statistician), Lou Sorrentino (head coach).

144

Coach: Ralph Thorne; Robert Lemke,
Chris Jasman, Tom Collier, Lyle Trumbull,
Chris Palmer, Jim O'Neill, Dave Eckman,
Amy Abbott, David Kramer.

Cheerleaders

Row 1: Louise Burchill, Susan Yeiter. Row 2: Judy Sargeant, Wendy Carter, Jean Krieg, Patty Mongon, Donna Hoffman.

Men's
Basketball

First Row: Paul Gouza, Dan Delp, Jim Foster, Jeff Bair, Pat Zlogar, Steve Weddle, Mark Sutovich, Rick Hoffman. **Second Row:**
ASSISTANT COACH: Al Haskowski, Brade Harmen, Jim Deer, Bob Johnston, Garry Freysinger, Greg Goodwin, Jon Spotto, Jo
Krolczyk, Jim Empfield, Fred Siebecker, COACH: Gordon Foster.

Women's Basketball

Jim Smith (coach), Miriam Hudecheck, Karen Reider, Dawn Adams, Deborah DeArrastia, Terri Eastwood, Laurie Kratzer, Betsy Spacek, Dicksie Boehler, Beth Anderson, Dave Kupp (asst. coach).

Wrestling

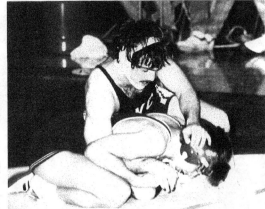

Dennis Delduco, Kevin Varano, Gary Reesor, Gerard Cappello, David Jones, John Ferrara, Steve Lenker, Terence O'Brien, Michael Rusen, Jeff Carter, Eric Kratzer, Wayne Meyer, Richard Kichman, Doug Sernoffsky, Steve Dyjak, Doug Rickenbach, Michael LaPorta. COACH: Gerald Petrofes.

Baseball

Frank Rhodes, Ron Robb, John Feaster, Tony Guasperini, John Parsons, Steve Nelson, Brian Cain, Bob Johnston, Talbot Barrow, Vaughn Robbins, Dave Williams, John Kiefel, Mark Smith, Dan Delp, Rich Bradley, Bob Fager, Scott Pontz, Mark Alexander. COACH: Ned Smith.

Men's Lacrosse

Tom Boyle, Bob Carson, Scott Cousin, Robert Dowd, John Gebhard, Dave Hall, John Herr, Randy Homan, Andy Jung, Joe Krolczyk, Chris McArdle, Bob McCallion, Wayne Meyer, Richard Miller, Joe Portolese, Michael Rusen, Paul Rusen, Jason S'braccia, Rick Shoff, Mike Sickler, Stan Sullivan, John Taddei, Rich Troutman, Rich Underwood, Marty Werkheiser. COACH: Bruce Correll.

Track

Jim O'Neill, Chris Palmer, Lyle Trumbul, Chris Jasman, Tom Collier, Bob Lemke, Dave Eckman. COACH: Ralph Thorn.

Women's
Lacrosse

Amy Abbott, Dawn Adams, Dawna Baker, Kristi Barbatschi, Amy Barefoot, Dicksie Boehler, Min
Cassell, Linda Emerson, Jenni Deardorff, Julie Gallo-Torres, Miriam Hudecheck, Sheila McElwe
Mary McNamara, Susan Newman. COACH: Janet Harriger.

So ends our play, but the story goes on. We all are on stage, each playing our part, making up the wonderful play called Life.

People leave and play their parts elsewhere, but the memories stay; while new actors come and change the scene.

Thank you, Lebanon Valley College, for helping us grow in the play of Life.

9 780428 368920